Healthy Foods

COOKING VEGGIES

SRI LANKAN STYLE

Recipes by Shyamali Perera

Series 2

Copyright

Copyright©2020 Shyamali Perera
All rights reserved

No part of this book may be used, reproduced, transmitted or sold in whole or part in any form (print or digital) without the written consent from the author.

All art work in this book, owned by Shyamali Perera. All photography credit to Shyamali Perera, Adobe Stock, BigStock, and Shutterstock royalty free stock photography.

Disclaimer

The material presented in this book is for informational purposes only. Please note that some ingredients mentioned in this book might not agree with first time users and food tasters.

Dedication

In loving memory of my dear Thatha, who passed away on February 13th, 2013. Thank you for giving me life, love, protection, knowledge and wisdom for 60 yrs.

Until we meet again on that beautiful shore

TABLE OF CONTENTS

INTRODUCTION 9

MIXED VEGETABLE CURRY 10

BONCHI CURRY (GREEN BEAN) 13

WAMBATU CURRY (EGGPLANT) 15

PARIPPU CURRY (YELLOW LENTIL) 17

ALA BADUN (DEVILED POTATO) 18

ALA KIRI HODI (YELLOW POTATO CURRY) 20

BEETROOT CURRY 22

ALU KEHEL CURRY (GREY BANANA) 24

BRINJAL MOJU (SWEET & SOUR EGGPLANT) 26

INNALA CURRY (SMALL POTATO) 28

WATTAKKA CURRY (PUMPKIN) 30

BANDAKKA BADUN (FRIED OKRA) 33

POLOS AMBUL (GREEN JAK FRUIT) 34

THAKKALI CURRY (TOMATO) 37

KADJU CURRY (CASHEW) 39

GOVA BADUN (FRIED CABBAGE) 40

HATHU CURRY (MUSHROOM) 43

ACKNOWLEDGMENTS 44

ABOUT THE AUTHOR 45

INTRODUCTION

Ayubowan. Sri Lanka is a pear-shaped island tucked away in the Indian Ocean, below India. To the seventh-century Arabian spice merchants, it was known as Serendip, and to the European conquerors and explorers, Ceylon or the Pearl of the Indian Ocean. Sri Lanka boasts of not only a variety of climates but also well-adapted cultural influences.

Sri Lanka's history dates before the time of the Buddha when the aboriginal tribes of the Yakkas and the Nagas ruled the land and were a part of the ancient Asian civilization. It is chronicled in the Mahawansa that the Buddha visited Sri Lanka on several occasions in the fifth century BC to preach to these tribes amidst their ongoing wars. Although Sri Lanka has fought many battles during the past 2500 years, the island has been blessed with tropical beauty, an abundance of food and rare aromatic spices. Folklore and folk tales depict, that these rare herbs and spices as being brought to the island by the demigod Hanuman for medicinal purposes during the great battle between Ravana, the Yakka king, and the Hindu deity Rama.

A variety of spices and herbs are used in Sri Lankan cooking. But the cooking styles have a marked difference according to the region of origin. The north and east of the country have cuisines with prominent south Indian flavors, and the hill country is flavored with hill-grown fruits and vegetables. The west and coastal areas boast of cuisines with an abundance of fresh fish and vegetables.

The use of these spices can be considered a personal style and preference; therefore, exact measurements and quantities are deemed unnecessary. Hence the Sri Lankan cook throws in a pinch of this and a pinch of that and wham-bam......the outcome is mouth-watering food, layered with a multitude of flavors. The famous Sri Lankan curry refers to a variety of flavorful dishes cooked mostly with coconut milk and is eaten usually with rice. The recipes in this book are written with an international audience in mind and can be changed to suit one's palate.

Hope you have a great culinary experience using these recipes.

MIXED VEGETABLE CURRY

Ingredients

- 3 potatoes
- 2 carrots
- ½ pound green beans
- 1 small cauliflower
- 1 large red bell pepper
- 2 onions chopped
- 1 sprig curry leaves
- 3 tomatoes chopped
- 6 garlic pods
- 1 tsp of curry powder
- 1 tsp of chili powder
- 1/4 cup chives
- 1 inch stick of cinnamon
- 1/4 tsp of turmeric powder
- 2 tbs of oil
- salt to taste

Directions

1. Cut all the vegetables finely. Heat oil in a pan and add the cut garlic, chopped onions, tomatoes, cinnamon, salt and fry for about 3 minutes.
2. Next add the cut vegetables and cook till the vegetables are crisp and soft. Add water if necessary.
3. Garnish with chopped chives.
4. Serve hot with rice or bread when ready.

BONCHI CURRY (GREEN BEAN)

Ingredients

- 1 packet of french cut beans
- pinch of pepper powder
- 1 onion chopped
- 1 tbs of oil
- 1 tsp red chili
- 1tsp curry powder
- 1/2 tsp turmeric powder
- salt to taste

Directions

1. Heat the oil and add the green beans and rest of the ingredients. Cook while mixing until the water has dried up and beans are tender.
2. Do not overcook to lose the color of the beans. Could be mixed with Maldive fish flakes if desired.

WAMBATU CURRY (EGGPLANT)

Ingredients

- 1 pound eggplant cut into strips
- 1 onion cut into small pieces
- 2 pods chopped garlic
- 3 slices chopped ginger
- 1 sprig curry leaves
- 2 tsp of curry powder
- 2 tsp of chili powder
- 1 tsp brown sugar
- 1 tsp of vinegar
- 1 cup of coconut milk
- 2 cups oil
- 1 inch stick of cinnamon
- 1 inch stick of lemon grass
- salt to taste

Method

1. Deep fry the eggplant strips and set them on a paper towel for the oil to drain.
2. Mix the rest of the ingredients with coconut milk and cook till the onions are cooked.
3. Next add the fried eggplant and simmer till the pieces absorb the gravy. Serve when hot.

PARIPPU CURRY (YELLOW LENTIL)

Ingredients

- 2 cups of yellow lentil soaked in water
- 1 onion chopped
- 5 pods garlic chopped
- 1 sprig curry leaves
- ¼ inch piece of cinnamon
- ½ tsp of turmeric powder
- 1 tbsp of oil
- ¼ tsp of fenugreek
- 1 tbsp of mustard seeds
- 10 dried red chilies broken into small pieces
- ½ cup coconut milk
- salt to taste

Method

1. Sauté the onions, garlic, curry leaves, cinnamon, fenugreek and the broken chili pieces.
2. When the onion mix becomes golden in color add the mustard seeds and let them pop.
3. Then add the lentil, turmeric powder coconut milk, salt and cook on a slow fire. Serve when lentils are soft and mushy.

ALA BADUN (DEVILED POTATO)

Ingredients

- 1 pound of potatoes
- 2 pounds of onions cut into thick rings
- 2 sprigs curry leaves
- 1 tbsp roasted chili flake
- 1 cup oil
- lime juice
- salt to taste

Directions

1. Add salt and boil the potatoes with the skin. Let it cool, skin the potatoes and cut them into cubes. Fry the cut onions with the curry leaves and salt.
2. When onions are fried and is turning into light brown add the potatoes with the chilies.
3. Lower the heat and cook for another 5 minutes. Lastly add the lime juice. Serve with roti or freshly baked bread.

ALA KIRI HODI (YELLOW POTATO CURRY)

Ingredients

- 1pound potatoes cut into uniform pieces
- 6 peppercorns
- 1 onion cut into small pieces
- 1 sprig curry Leaves
- 1 inch stick of cinnamon
- 1 cup of coconut milk
- 1 tsp of fenugreek
- ¼ tsp of turmeric powder
- salt to taste

Directions

1. Cook the cut potatoes (in enough water to cover them) along with the rest of the ingredients except the coconut milk.
2. When the potatoes are cooked and soft add the coconut milk and bring to boil.
3. Add the peppercorns and salt to taste when potatoes are tender and well simmered. Serve hot.

BEETROOT CURRY

Ingredients

- 3 mid size beetroots
- 2 shallots chopped finely
- 1 clove garlic chopped finely
- 1 geen chili chopped finely
- 1 sprig curry leaves
- 1 inch pandan leaf
- 1 tsp chili powder
- 1 tsp roasted curry powder
- 1/2 tsp cumin powder
- 1/4 tsp turmeric powder
- 1/2 cup light coconut milk
- 1/4 cup thick coconut milk
- salt to taste

Directions

1. Wash and peel the beetroots. Cut into lengthwise thin 1 inch strips.
2. Mix all the ingredients with the light coconut milk, cut beetroot, and cook till the coconut milk is absorbed to the beetroot.
3. Then add the thick coconut milk, cover pan and cook on a low fire till the beetroots are soft, the gravy is thick and simmered.

Note

- The cut beetroots can bleed and will leave stains.

ALU KEHEL CURRY (GREY BANANA)

Ingredients

- 4 big raw grey bananas
- 4 onions
- 6 pods garlic
- 3 slices of ginger
- ¼ tsp of turmeric powder
- 1 tbs of curry powder
- 1 tsp fenugreek
- 1 sprig curry leaves
- 1 cup of coconut milk
- 2 cups oil to fry bananas
- salt to taste

Directions

1. Skin and cut the bananas into small cubes and fry them till golden brown. Leave to drain.
2. Mix the rest of the ingredients with the coconut milk and cook till the gravy boils.
3. Add the fried bananas and simmer till the gravy turns thick and grey.
4. Serve with roti or rice.

Gray Bananas

BRINJAL MOJU (SWEET & SOUR EGGPLANT)

Ingredients

- 1 pound eggplant
- 1/4 pound green pepper
- 1/4 pound shallots
- 2 pods garlic
- 3 slices ginger
- 1 cup oil
- 1 tbsp vinegar
- 1 tsp sugar
- ½ tsp turmeric powder
- 1 tsp ground mustard paste
- salt to taste

Directions

1. Slice the eggplant and green pepper lengthwise. Clean the shallots, crush the garlic and shred the ginger. Heat the oil and fry eggplant slices until browned. Remove, drain and set aside.
2. In the same oil lightly fry the green pepper and shallots and when soft, drain and set aside. Drain off half the oil and add garlic, ginger, vinegar, salt, turmeric and mustard paste to the pan and cook for 2-3 minutes.
3. Add the fried eggplant slices, green pepper and shallots and cook for a further 5minutes. Just prior to serving stir in the sugar and salt to taste. Make sure all the ingredients are well coated.

INNALA CURRY (SMALL POTATO)

Ingredients

- 1 pound innala
- 2 big onions
- 3 pods garlic
- 1 sprig curry Leaves
- A few chopped cilantro leaves
- ¼ inch piece of cinnamon
- 1 cup thick coconut milk
- 1 tsp of chili powder
- 1 tsp of curry powder
- ¼ tsp of turmeric powder
- 2 tbsp of oil
- 2 tbsp of lemon juice
- 1 tsp of fenugreek
- salt to taste

Directions

1. Boil the innala and peel the skins, and set aside. Chop the onions and garlic finely.
2. Heat oil and fry onions, garlic, curry leaves, cinnamon and fenugreek. Add the curry, chili, turmeric powders and salt to the mix and fry for a few more minutes.
3. Then add the peeled innala and thick coconut milk to the fried ingredients and let simmer.
4. Lastly add the lemon juice, and garnish with cilantro leaves. Serve with rice, bread or roti

Innala (Small Potato)

WATTAKKA CURRY (PUMPKIN)

Ingredients

- 1 pound kabocha pumpkin
- 2 shallots chopped finely
- 1 green chili chopped finely
- 2 cloves garlic
- 1 slice ginger
- 1/2 tsp turmeric powder
- 1/2 tsp pepper powder
- 1 tsp mustard seeds
- 1/2 cup grated coconut
- 1/2 cup light coconut milk
- 1/2 cup thick coconut milk
- 1 sprig curry leaves
- 1 inch pandan leaf
- 1 inch cinnamon stick
- 1/4 cup water
- salt to taste

Directions

1. Wash and cut the pumpkin into cubes with the skin. Cook the cut pumpkins in the light coconut milk with the shallots, green chili, cinnamon, curry leaves, pandan leaf, turmeric powder and salt.
2. While the pumpkin is cooking, grind the grated coconut, mustard seeds, pepper powder, ginger and garlic with 1/4 cup water to form a paste.
3. Dissolve the paste in the thick coconut milk and add to the pumpkin. Lower the heat and cook till the gravy simmers and is fragrant.

BANDAKKA BADUN (FRIED OKRA)

Ingredients

- 1 pound of okra cut into small pieces at an angle
- 1 onion
- 1 cut tomato
- 1 lime juice
- 1 sprig curry leaves
- 1 tsp chili powder
- 1 tsp of curry powder
- 1/2 tsp turmeric powder
- 1 tbs of oil
- salt to taste

Directions

1. Wash the cut okra in lime juice to take away the slime. Heat the oil, and cook the okra and the rest of the ingredients in the oil.
2. When simmered well, add salt, curry powder, chili powder, turmeric powder and cook for another 5 minutes till the okra pieces are soft.
3. Remove from fire and sprinkle lime juice. Serve while hot.

POLOS AMBUL (GREEN JAK FRUIT)

Ingredients

- 1 can green jak fruit
- 2 shallots chopped finely
- 2 cloves garlic chopped finely
- 1 piece ginger chopped finely
- 1 sprig curry leaves
- 1 inch pandan leaf
- 6 dried red chili
- 1 tsp mustard seeds
- 1 tsp chili powder
- 1 tsp roasted curry powder
- 1/2 tsp turmeric powder
- 1 tbs tamarind juice
- 1 cup thick coconut milk
- 1/4 cup of oil
- salt to taste

Directions

1. Drain the liquid from the jak fruit pieces. Cut pieces into halves. Heat oil and add the finely chopped onions, ginger, garlic, curry leaves, pandan leaf, and fry till the onions turn golden brown. Then add the dry red chili, mustard seeds and fry for 1 minute.
2. Reduce heat and add the jak fruit pieces, curry powder, chili powder, turmeric powder, salt and tamarind juice. Mix well.
3. Lastly add the coconut milk and cook on low heat for about 1 hour till the jak fruit pieces are soft and a bit flaky.

Note

- 2 pieces of Goraka- Garcinia Cambogia can be used as a substitute for tamarind juice in this recipe.
- Flaked jak fruit could be used as a filling for a vegan taco.

THAKKALI CURRY (TOMATO)

Ingredients

- 1 pound tomatoes
- 2 large onions
- 6 green chilies
- 1 sprig curry leaves
- 2 tbsp of sugar
- 1 tbsp of curry powder
- ¼ tsp of turmeric powder
- 1 cup coconut milk
- salt to taste

Directions

1. Cut all the tomatoes into big pieces. Mix all the ingredients with the coconut milk and add to the tomatoes. Cook on a slow fire till tomatoes are soft.
2. Serve with rice bread or roti when ready.

KADJU CURRY (Cashew)

Ingredients

- 1 pound of whole cashews
- 1 whole onion cut into cubes
- 1 tbsp of curry powder
- 1 tbsp of chili powder
- ¼ tsp of fenugreek
- 1/4 tsp of turmeric powder
- 1 tbsp of oil
- ½ inch piece of cinnamon
- 1 cup thick coconut milk
- 1 sprig curry leaves
- salt to taste

Directions

1. Soak the cashews in water for half an hour. Fry the onions, curry leaves, cinnamon stick and fenugreek till fragrant. Then add curry chili, turmeric powders and salt.
2. Add the drained cashews and stir well to mix.
3. Mix the cup of thick coconut milk with a little water and add to the cashew curry. Cook on low for 10 minutes. Serve when cashews are tender and cooked.
4. Do not make the coconut milk mixture too watery.

GOVA BADUN (FRIED CABBAGE)

Ingredients

- 1/2 head of white cabbage
- 3 shallots chopped finely
- 2 green chillies chopped finely
- 2 cloves garlic chopped finely
- 1/4 tsp turmeric powder
- 1/4 tsp chili powder
- 1/4 tsp of fennel seeds
- 1 sprig curry leaves
- 1 inch pandan leaf
- 1/2 inch stick cinnamon
- 1/4 cup oil
- salt to taste

Directions

1. Wash and shred the cabbage finely. Heat the oil and fry the chopped shallots, green chili, garlic, curry leaves, pandan leaf and cinnamon stick.
2. When onions turn light golden brown and fragrant, add the shredded cabbage and continue to fry.
3. Then add the chili powder, turmeric powder and salt and fry till the cabbages are crisp and a bit crunchy. Serve while hot.

HATHU CURRY (MUSHROOM)

Ingredients

- 1 pound mushrooms
- 1 red, green and yellow peppers
- 1 onion
- 2 pods garlic
- 3 slices ginger
- 1 tsp of curry powder
- 1 tsp of chili powder
- 1 tbsp of oil
- 1 lime juice
- salt to taste

Directions

1. Wash and cut the mushrooms, bell peppers, onions, ginger and garlic.
2. Heat the oil and add the cut ingredients and cook in very high heat for 5 minutes.
3. Then add the chili and curry powders and cook for a further 5 minutes.
4. Sprinkle the lime juice and serve when mushrooms are cooked and tender.

ACKNOWLEDGMENTS

Writing a book is harder than I thought and more rewarding than I could have ever imagined. None of this would have been possible without my awesome 86 yr old mother, Nalini Perera. She was the narrator for this series of Sri Lankan recipes during our mandatory quarantine for the COVID-19 pandemic of 2020.

Thank you to my younger brother Gamini Perera, who took the time, and effort to gather and preserve important family history, so it could be passed down to our next generations, and for always sharing childhood memories when we speak.

A big thank you to my book designer Alexey Larentev of PhotoMagLab in Ukraine. His tireless efforts and creativity made it possible for me to publish this collection of authentic recipes books.

Above all, I'm eternally grateful for and thankful to my family: Manjula, Michael, Mikaile, Manjari, Mychal, Charith, Tracy, Ari, Suren, Diana and Freddie. You have always given me a reason to take the next step forward.

ABOUT THE AUTHOR

Shyamali Perera was born in Colombo, Sri Lanka, and emigrated to the United States in 1989, during Sri Lanka's civil war. She was an educator of young children for thirty years in Orange County, California. Her first book Curry & Rice was published as a Mother's Day gift in 2007 and was later published as an e-book in 2014. Since then she has published several cookbooks and children's books available in both ebook and paperback versions. Shyamali is also an amateur photographer and likes to create beautiful books with inspiring ideas. Presently, she lives with her family in Southern California and continues to dedicate her time to writing a variety of cookbooks and children's books.

www.ingramcontent.com/pod-product-compliance
Lightning Source LLC
Chambersburg PA
CBHW041435010526
44118CB00002B/76